GW00787586

*Quick*GUIDES
everything you need to know...fast

Fundraising From Individuals

by Adrienne Hall

reviewed by Jacqui Scott

WIREMILL
PUBLISHING LTD

Across the world the organizations and institutions that fundraise to finance their work are referred to in many different ways. They are charities, non-profits or not-for-profit organizations, non-governmental organizations (NGOs), voluntary organizations, academic institutions, agencies, etc. For ease of reading, we have used the term Nonprofit Organization, Organization or NPO as an umbrella term throughout the *Quick*Guide series. We have also used the spellings and punctuation used by the author.

Published by
Wiremill Publishing Ltd.
Edenbridge, Kent TN8 5PS, UK
info@wiremillpublishing.com
www.wiremillpublishing.com
www.quickguidesonline.com

British Library Cataloguing in Publication Data
A catalogue record for this book is available from the British Library.

ISBN Number 1-905053-13-4

Printed by Rhythm Consolidated Berhad, Malaysia
Cover Design by Jennie de Lima and Edward Way
Design by Colin Woodman Design

Disclaimer of Liability
The author, reviewer and publisher shall have neither liability nor responsibility to any person or entity with respect to any loss or damage caused or alleged to be caused directly or indirectly by the information contained in this book. While the book is as accurate as possible, there may be errors, omissions or inaccuracies.

CONTENTS

FUNDRAISING FROM INDIVIDUALS

INTRODUCTION

There are three sources of income for nonprofit organisations (NPOs): *earned income* (revenue from products and services), *public sources* (government) and *private sources* (grantmaking trusts and foundations, corporations and individuals). For most NPOs, the majority of donations come from individuals.

Engaging individuals in your fundraising programmes will usually be the single most important factor in achieving your targets. The impact of the initial contact and the quality of subsequent ones will determine the nature of the overall relationship and the degree of trust between your NPO and the individuals who support it. Inducing individuals to choose your organisation over others and encouraging them to increase the frequency and size of their gifts are the key challenges. This Guide aims to give you the tools to meet those challenges.

There are six steps in an individual fundraising programme, all of which will be discussed in this Guide. They are:

- Identify
- Interest
- Involve
- Ask (and receive)
- Thank
- Renew

Some steps may be combined. For example, an enquiry or gift coming through a website or from other publicity indicates someone who is both *identified* and *interested*.

While the Guide focuses on individuals as donors, it is important to remember also that fundraising from companies, trusts, foundations or any funding body means engaging the individuals who represent those organisations. Some of the techniques covered here can be used in those situations as well. "People give to people" is a truism and worth remembering.

When planning an individual donor programme, the planning canvas can be as varied as individuals themselves. You need a system to organise, manage and track the programme's progress. To do this, *understand your objectives* and create a system that enables you to *measure your results against them*.

The aim of an individual donor programme is to encourage people to give to you, keep them giving, and increase the size of their contributions.

Reviewer's Comment
Some definitions are helpful at this stage. An individual donor programme is the planned process by which an organisation encourages donors to increase the value of their gifts over time, through mailings, calls, incentives, meetings, or other means. (This is also sometimes called an individual giving programme or donor development programme.)

Lifetime value or long-term value is the total amount of money a donor gives to an organisation over the duration of his/her involvement – which is hoped to be over a donor's lifetime!

The Donor Loyalty Ladder
An effective way to structure the programme and measure its success is the "loyalty ladder." The idea is taken from the for-profit sector, where it is used to measure customer loyalty and company effectiveness.

Donor Loyalty Ladder
Adapted for Development

- Suspect
- Prospect
- Donor
- High Value Donor
- Advocate

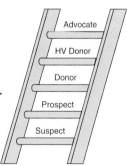

Beerstecher Hall Consulting

Continues on next page

The loyalty ladder has five rungs:

1. **Suspects** – people who have some contact with your organisation.

2. **Prospects** – people who pay attention.

3. **Donors** – people who give.

4. **High value donors** – loyal, regular donors who increase the value of their gifts.

5. **Advocates** – donors who promote your cause, ask others to give, and participate in many ways in the life of your organisation.

Your aim is to move people up the ladder. In this way, you can increase the lifetime value of each donor while minimising costs, so that a lower proportion of revenues are swallowed up by administration.

Reviewer's Comment
Terminology varies in different countries, though the principles are the same. I would use "cold prospects" for people who have never supported an organisation before (i.e., people targeted in a mailing) and "warm prospects" or just "prospects" for people who have already had some contact with the organisation.

It can be shown that it costs three times as much money to find a new donor as it does to keep an existing one, and it costs 30 times as much to attract a new donor yourself as to have an existing donor find a new one for you. That's why you should try to build loyalty with donors to the point that they start to work for you.

There is, of course, a balance to keep. You don't want to exhaust donors by focussing all your attention on them, but you don't want to lose them by not paying them enough attention. You need continually to attract new people to your programme as well as increase the number of repeat donations from those already involved.

Identifying who might support you is determined by what "you" are as an organisation: why you exist and what value you add to society. Those who share your values, find your mission credible and trust you to deliver on it are the people who are going to support you. Those who have some personal and emotional connection to your activities are most likely to want to become involved.

The first milestone is a clearly stated vision, mission and objective statement outlining your *case for support*, which is framed as a powerful *invitation to invest*.

How you get the message across about what you do, why and how you do it, and who benefits need not be hugely expensive, involving glossy publications or advertising placements. The message should effectively communicate what makes you distinctive (your "brand"), be rich in thought and content, and be as appropriate as possible in presentation.

If possible, invest in the expertise of a creative agency to get the message right and limit production costs. Make sure your message converts easily from one medium to another – direct mail, fax, the web, radio, TV, and print advertising – and that it is consistent across all media.

Reviewer's Comment
Using an agency does cost money. Provided it is managed well, it is money well spent and can mean savings on other things (like staff time). Using an agency can increase the response rate significantly.

If your NPO is a global organisation or has multinational or multicultural markets, ensure your marketing concepts translate correctly into other languages or cultures. What might be a "hit" concept in one culture could be wholly inappropriate in another.

There are a variety of methods available to identify potential individual donors to your organisation. They include the following.

The Web
The web provides a reasonably inexpensive way of reaching a large number of people. The first step is

Continues on next page

usually to establish a website for your organisation. It needn't be fancy with lots of gimmicks, but it does need to be appropriate for your organisation.

When creating your website, remember that visitors to a web page decide whether to stay in less than three seconds. Your message has to attract their attention in that time. The success of any website depends on keeping visitors aware of its existence and constantly engaging the visitor.

If your organisation does not have the facilities, budget or technical resources to create its own website, look instead for organisations that offer inexpensive or free web pages to nonprofit organisations. Increasingly, being on the web is an important component of the individual fundraising mix.

Direct Mail
Where resources permit, start shaping your message using the web as a basis. If the message is punchy and powerful on the web, it should work to good effect in print and other media.

Reviewer's Comment
Although the web is a huge growth area, even now many organisations are more reliant on mail and telephone (and other "traditional" methods) for fundraising from individuals, probably because NPOs are still so reliant on "traditional" donors. Most organisations still create the message in print and in person, and then translate it to the web.

For those wishing to expand their mailing base or to create new operations, good quality data-guaranteed mailing lists can be bought from a wide variety of sources. The web is the most easily accessible source of mailing-list providers, or a direct marketing agency may offer lists as well as do creative work.

Reviewer's Comment
You should make yourself aware of any regulatory frameworks that may exist in your country for mailing preferences, by which people can opt out of receiving certain types of mail.

Quality mailing lists enable you to personalise your letter and message. Individual fundraising is a people-based game, and your communications need to reflect that; you want prospects to know you have taken time to get their personal details right. The skill of effective direct marketing is developing a pack that combines the right message with the right people at the right time.

Advertising

A well-planned and cost-effective media campaign is essential to building your brand. It is a key element in managing perceptions about who you are and communicating your message in the way that you want.

Reviewer's Comment

Advertising is also a vital donor-acquisition tool when combining editorial content with advertisements that include donation response mechanisms. ("Donor acquisition" is activity aimed at recruiting new donors to support a cause. In many larger organisations, it is a fundraising discipline in its own right.)

Public Relations

Your relationship with print and electronic media – how they report on your cause – is important in determining public perceptions of your organisation. Advertising is your message as you want it said. But information and opinion communicated by news media through reporters, writers and editors are potentially more credible and therefore stronger.

It is vital to build good relationships with people in the media, to treat them with respect, to give them correct information (they're sure to find out if you don't), and to use them to get your message out to the public without paying advertising rates.

Networks

Networks are another way of identifying and cementing links with people who might want to support you. They can differ from broader membership programmes, in that they are most effectively created for individuals who have a specific interest and goal in mind. Networks have the potential to increase your prospect pool in specific categories of potential

Continues on next page

donors, particularly at the major-gift level, and can be an effective tool in building a relationship with them.

Rich Lists
A rich list is a method of identifying high net-worth individuals (and their family grantmaking bodies). However, it is a common mistake to assume that just because people are rich, they want, or should want, to make a (large) gift. NPOs get most of their money from individuals of relatively modest means. Nevertheless, major-gift prospects have the power to make "transformational" gifts – those that are so large as to significantly alter the future of an organisation and its delivery capacity.

High net-worth individuals often establish grantmaking bodies (trusts and foundations) through which to make charitable gifts. This method often has tax advantages and provides protection from unwanted approaches, by establishing clear donation policies and "gatekeepers" who administer the grantmaking body.

Events
Events present fundraisers with many opportunities to target individuals. As well as raising money, they provide ways to identify people interested in your cause, to use celebrities and bring your NPO into the public eye, to cement the support of current donors, and to engage the interest of major-gift prospects. They offer occasions for publicity and image building. They can achieve these objectives, however, only if properly managed.

The type of event you choose – a dinner, golf tournament, marathon run, yacht race, concert, or auction – will depend on the kind of work you do and what phase of the development programme you have reached.

Celebrities can bring profile and publicity to your NPO. They need to be used with care, however, and with an eye on the profile you want to promote.

Reviewer's Comment
Any event that depends entirely on celebrity involvement is risky. Ideally an event should be able to stand alone if the celebrity concerned is unable to attend at the last minute.

Having identified potential donors through the various methods outlined previously, you will want to involve them in your organisation as well as ask them for a donation. In some cases, involvement in your organisation will be a higher priority and a valuable long-term investment both for you and for your potential donor.

Membership Programmes
A membership programme is a way to induce individuals to get involved and therefore expand the potential donor base.

Membership programmes can move people up the loyalty ladder. They are not, strictly, gift-raising programmes but an important part of identifying interested people and creating fertile soil to turn their support into gifts. But membership benefits and donor benefits need to be distinct, clearly defined and communicated across your media mix. Membership programmes, if they are fee-paying and not cautiously managed, can undercut income from gift-raising programmes. Membership fees may be confused with gift support and also may carry no tax advantages for the individual or the organisation.

Volunteers
Inviting people to become involved in your programmes on a voluntary basis is an important way to engage individuals. Volunteers can lead and coordinate groups, organise events, join boards, help with care, and participate in many other activities. Involvement of this kind gives individuals a way to expand their horizons, their networks and their experience, and to act as ambassadors for your organisation at the same time. Making the experience as positive as possible for volunteers will maintain loyalty and will encourage others in their network of friends, colleagues and associates to become involved as well. Importantly, it will increase your prospect base – people whose support you can solicit and who are likely to respond positively to an approach.

Donor Research
Having identified potential donors, it is important to know about them. Prospect/donor profiling is an essential and specialised area of fundraising. Once you have a list of people identified through some of the activities previously mentioned, you need to understand all you can about them in

Continues on next page

order to identify those individuals who might become larger donors, who might become involved in your organisation through volunteering or membership programmes, or who might be asked to serve on your governing body.

Apart from the basic information covering contact details (personal and business), NPOs need to create sophisticated profiles of individuals whom they want to engage and approach, particularly for large gifts.

For example, consider researching:

- Levels of wealth.
- Professional or business information.
- Personal and family interests and passions.
- Personal and family histories.
- Values.
- Other causes they have supported.

- Whether their wealth is inherited or self-made.
- Whether they are "asset rich" but "cash poor".
- What share options and/or directorships they hold.

These are all indicators of what they might be interested in and what gift level might be appropriate.

Reviewer's Comment
Individual charities must make their own decisions on how to approach their research needs, but they may do their own desk research through bought directories, the web and newspapers, or they may outsource it to direct marketing or specialist research agencies. This level of research is appropriate to identify prospects who can give above a certain level; it is clearly not necessary to gather this level of detail about all donors.

Asking (and Receiving)

Some asking is indirect. The web, volunteer activities and events are all ways in which individuals support an organisation without being directly asked to do so. Other times, the potential donor is specifically asked for a donation. For small donations, this may be, for example, through a direct mail campaign in which the donor is sent material and asked to respond by mail, telephone, or online. For larger donations and the most specialised campaigns, the asking will be personal, including telephone fundraising and face-to-face meetings.

Telephone Fundraising (Telethons/Phonathons)

There are many specialist companies set up to run telephone campaigns, and it may be appropriate to run your campaign through one of them rather than in-house, particularly if you don't have the staff or volunteers to undertake this activity. When choosing such a company, make sure that you fully understand its history and success patterns. Some research into its client base is also advisable.

Reviewer's Comment
There is a risk inherent in outsourcing telephone campaigns. A "bad" call could lose a donor forever. No matter how well you train and monitor the callers, outsourcing means losing some degree of control.

Asking by telephone has several advantages. It brings you into direct contact with individuals and enables you to research and build your intelligence base about the way you are perceived and why people might (or might not) support you. It also provides an opportunity for the donor to build a relationship with the NPO through personal contact.

There are disadvantages to the telephone approach. Some people equate it with pressure selling or an intrusion in their home, both of which are why well-managed telethons will always mail a letter before the campaign, offering people the option not to be called. Do be aware of cultural and social issues regarding this as well as all methods.

Continues on next page

However, it is incumbent on fundraisers to be aware of any regulatory frameworks that may exist, through which people can opt out of receiving unsolicited telephone calls.

Face-to-Face

There are two main types of asking for funding in person. One is the broadest possible, the other the most personal:

- "Chugging" is when people are approached on the street by hired hands, often students or casual workers. Although this method may produce significant funds, some NPOs find it can generate hostility rather than support. However, many NPOs still find it their best donor-acquisition method in terms of cost-effectiveness and return on investment.

- A request at a meeting, which takes place by arrangement between a prospect and a fundraiser/CEO/senior volunteer representing the NPO, is the method necessary for large donations and major-donor prospects. Such meetings require careful planning and skills training for the NPO staff concerned. You should have researched the prospects and be thoroughly informed of their personal, business and financial circumstances, as well as what might encourage them to donate.

There are many ways you can receive donations.

Regular Giving

Regular giving programmes enable your organisation to have the resources needed for its day-to-day business. Building up a solid base of steady donors ensures that you can plan ahead and identify gaps for other fundraising efforts. Retaining the loyalty of annual givers means that even if a donor does not increase in amount or frequency, over time she or he will become a higher value donor.

Special Gifts

Special gifts are usually one-off gifts toward a particular project. Don't be shy about asking annual or regular givers to make a special gift from time to time for a special project. If you have looked after them well and they care enough about your cause, they are quite likely to support you.

Reviewer's Comment

Many charities ask donors several times each year for more donations, sometimes with a specific project in mind, and other times just as an emotive appeal about their work.

Major Gifts

Major gifts are those gifts that can significantly increase your capacity as an organisation to deliver on its mission. A major gift can be an endowment that is invested to produce revenue on an annual basis, a donation of equipment or other property, or simply a large donation.

Leadership Gifts

Leadership gifts are donations that, because of their source or size, can transform the future and direction of an organisation by creating and sustaining a development in perpetuity. Examples might be a new hospital wing, a new library, an aircraft to an aid charity, or a community centre. Leadership gifts can also be the first or one of the main donations in a capital, or other, campaign. They can be important as a means of encouraging other donations.

All giving contributes to your brand – how people see you. Leadership gifts are especially important in this respect because they demonstrate faith in the organisation's cause and, as importantly, its leadership.

Reviewer's Comment

A word of caution, though: it is important that the donation is given in accordance with the aims of the charity and does not lead the NPO to begin work outside the remit of its stated aims and objectives, in order to meet the conditions of this additional income.

Revenue or Endowment Giving

This is a common distinction. Revenue income means those donations to be spent directly. Endowment gifts are invested as capital, with the interest on the capital to be spent.

Continues on next page

Venture Philanthropy

With the rise of entrepreneurship and the entrepreneurial ethos, venture philanthropy is a growing field. It applies to endowment gifts and means, in essence, that the donor retains ownership of the gift, or the capital sum; he or she renews the pledge to donate the interest on that sum on the basis of certain performance criteria.

Bequests/Legacies

Legacy (or bequest, the words mean the same) fundraising is an unpredictable but significant part of any individual giving programme. Legacies are gifts at death. Immortality is a motivator in legacy giving, and rewards (both recognition and tax benefits) that recognise this should be a credible and visible element in your programme.

Reviewer's Comment

Sometimes NPOs find that they do not benefit from the final Will, even after having been told that they would. This may be because the donor changed his or her mind or because his or her circumstances changed.

Tax-Efficient Giving

Tax laws can encourage gifts and are an important revenue generator for NPOs as well as for donors who want to make a gift in a tax-efficient manner. Negotiating a gift that meets this requirement requires you to know your tax law.

Ensure that your printed material covers tax aspects and addresses the tax benefits to you and your donor. Consult a professional to ensure that your understanding is correct and to check that your giving literature conforms to tax laws.

New Methods of Giving

Fundraising methods are increasing because the business sector and companies are continually inventing new ways for individuals to support organisations. Following are some of these innovative ideas, but do look locally to see what else is available.

Texting
This is a relatively new service being offered to fundraisers by mobile phone donation services. Requests for funds are sent out to people's mobile phones.

ASKING (AND RECEIVING)

Foreign Currency

Organisations exchange foreign currency change into support for charity organisations. They collect on aircraft and other outlets where people might be carrying unwanted foreign currency in coins and small notes.

Online Shopping

An online shop raises money from your supporters' online purchases. Participating retailers pay a percentage of the purchase price back to your organisation.

Credit Cards

Credit card companies give NPOs the option to offer the people on their databases a dedicated credit card whereby the credit card company pays a percentage of transaction value to the NPO.

Reviewer's Comment
Companies that provide these services can be found online, through directories, by recommendation from NPO contacts, or via advertisements in publications aimed at fundraisers.

Solicitation plans implement the steps of fundraising and the tools of the trade, both discussed previously with regard to individual donors.

The most important ingredient of the solicitation plan is an understanding of the prospects you are engaging – what they care about, what their personal and family histories are, what their connections are between your organisation's values and their lives, what other organisations they support, what they want as recognition for their support.

This understanding will enable you to decide whether, for example, they would prefer an invitation to host a dinner with a celebrity; having a one-on-one meeting with your chief executive to discuss your organisation, its objectives and strategy; or getting hands-on experience of what you do (a ward tour for a hospital or a backstage tour for a performing arts organisation, for example). The greater their involvement is, the higher the potential value of the gift.

The Giving Pyramid

It is useful to divide suspects, prospects and donors into categories for planning and management purposes. The "giving pyramid" is a common way of doing this. The giving levels can be adapted according to what is appropriate for your NPO.

Whether identifying individuals as "suspects" or as "prospects," it is helpful to understand their giving potential and to categorise them using the giving pyramid. Once they have become donors, you can measure their gift levels against the categories you have given them, for purposes of evaluation and solicitation planning.

The giving pyramid also provides excellent visual assistance when you're creating a solicitation plan. The desired result is to move donors from one level to another. Your donor base may include a multimillionaire, a high earning corporate executive without children, a teacher with a family, and a widow with an inheritance. All may begin their relationship with the organisation at the bottom of the pyramid. The solicitation plan may determine that the multimillionaire could end at the top of the pyramid, the corporate executive would be an appropriate target for major gifts, the teacher with limited resources would make a regular and committed giver, and the widow with an inheritance could be a candidate for special gifts.

Plotting this on the pyramid can help you make the plan more effective and appropriate for each donor.

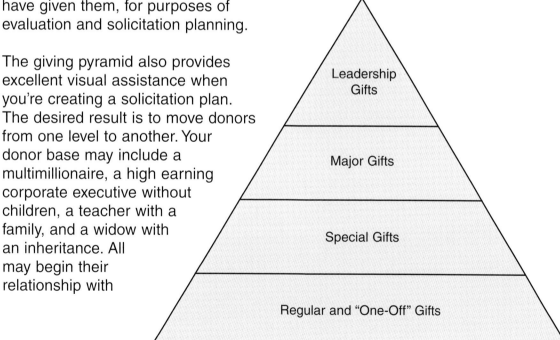

Leadership Gifts

Major Gifts

Special Gifts

Regular and "One-Off" Gifts

Your database is your "people base." It records and manages all the individuals you want to engage or you have engaged. It makes possible: identifying, interesting, involving, asking and receiving and, ultimately, thanking and renewing.

How the database is organised is key to effective programming and measurement. Segmenting the database into the five categories on the loyalty ladder is a helpful way of dividing individuals into manageable groups, based on the stage of your relationship and the activities you are implementing for each group. You can then measure the effectiveness of those activities by tracking the movement of people between categories, as well as monitoring retention rates (i.e., how many donors you keep).

Reviewer's Comment
Segmenting can be defined as making a selection of contacts based on common criteria and separating these contacts from the rest of the database, perhaps for purposes of a targeted mailing.

As well as segmenting by loyalty ladder, I find it useful to segment by acquisition channel (i.e., the means by which individuals were recruited, such as mailings, telephone campaigns, face-to-face). Donors tend to be different depending on the way they were recruited. Face-to-face (or direct dialogue) is a classic example because donors are frequently impossible to later contact by telephone and they never respond by mail! It is also useful to segment by recency, frequency and value of gift. Your database should allow you to segment using several selection criteria.

There are a number of custom-built databases on the market for fundraising organisations. Choosing the right one is very important to the success of your programme.

The right database must ensure that you can:

- Segment individuals into manageable groups.

- Hold all the information you need (for example, all contact details, gift type, amount, appeals responded to, preferred means of contact, etc.).

Keeping Track (Your Database)

- Prompt and track activities and responses to them.

- Track individual donor histories and income.

- Forecast giving income.

- Generate accurate financial reports.

- Generate management reports (how many new donors, how many lapsed donors, how many donors increasing gifts, responses to marketing initiatives, profiles of people responding and not responding, and so on).

- Track and compare responses to marketing initiatives.

- Prompt mailings (acknowledgments, receipts, invitations).

These are the basic specifications. A database that fails to meet your needs represents money wasted through a rise in hidden costs, damaged relationships (where incorrect data, tracking or reporting means you get your communications wrong), and failure to provide management the information needed for an effective and efficient operation.

When specifying what you want from a system, be careful that available packages and, in particular, the level of after-sales customer support match your needs. Some NPOs commission custom-built databases. This is a viable option, provided the contract with the database writer is clearly binding with regard to any failures, and the documentation is sufficiently comprehensive for the system to be maintained later by people other than its designer.

Agencies can be engaged to analyse your data – spot patterns and trends in giving and their relationship to activities and promotions. They can prove to be a worthwhile investment for segmenting your database and improving return on investment forecasts.

If you are a small organisation or one with few resources, don't feel the need to go out and purchase an expensive system. Anything is better than nothing, and, if necessary, even a simple database can grow as you do.

Thanking the people who support you is the single most important aspect of your engagement with individuals. Many organisations make the mistake of setting a fundraising target, getting the money through the door and then forgetting to follow up, thank and sustain relationships with the people who made that possible.

They forget that what they have received is not money but "gifts." People become donors when they choose to support you. A plethora of organisations are competing for gifts from individuals. Undervaluing the choice people make in selecting your organisation rather than another is extremely shortsighted and will not make for long-term viability (or build your donors' lifetime value).

Find at least three methods of thanking individual donors for their gifts. Emails, letters or promotional gifts are common ways of doing this. Encourage a corporate sponsor to underwrite an event to thank and update the donors on your campaign and your progress. Simple gestures such as naming donors on your website and in your annual reports and newsletters indicate that you appreciate the support they have given. Create an "in memoriam" site to mark legacies and to enable donors to commemorate, by supporting your programme, those who have been important to them.

Reviewer's Comment

In some cultures, promotional gifts are often not well received by many donors. They may perceive that the organisation is spending money on gimmicks rather than on the work that their gifts were intended to fund.

Keep donors informed about what your organisation is doing and the progress that their support has made possible. Do not be afraid to ask again, but do ensure that they also receive communications from you that do not make another "ask."

MEASURING YOUR EFFECTIVENESS

There are two measurements for assessing your programme's effectiveness – quantitative and qualitative. Use both. Quantitative measurements usually ask, "Did we get enough gifts to meet our targets?" They should also look at how much you invested to get the gifts and whether your targeted return on investment was met. Qualitative measurements assess the number of new donors added to the database, individual donor value, donor retention rates, growth in gift size, the effectiveness of each of your programmes at donor acquisition and retention. Focussing purely on quantitative measurements without qualitative donor growth targets can be one of the most destructive things NPOs do to their effectiveness and credibility in the long term.

Giving your programme structure by identifying people in terms of the loyalty ladder and the giving pyramid and having this information supported on your database will mean that you can track and measure the quality of your programme.

"**Moves Management**" is a process taken from marketing and can be effectively applied to fundraising situations. If you have structured your database as previously discussed, you can set goals for yourself with each of the individuals on your database and understand when they respond positively and notice when they lapse. You can track how successful you are at moving them up the ladder and the pyramid, and you can determine which aspects of your programme are most effective in doing this. This process also provides an action plan for your fundraising team and an effective measure of success.

It is important to bring in gifts and meet your objectives at minimum cost. This does not mean zero investment in your programme. It means that you are managing the investment in your efforts well and can understand where to invest and where to disinvest in activities. Measuring the return on investment against targets is critical to these decisions.

FINAL THOUGHTS

An individual giving programme can and should be as rich, innovative and varied as individuals and organisations.

- ■ Understand your objectives.

- ■ Communicate your vision, values and mission.

- ■ Create a compelling message.

- ■ Know your prospects and donors.

- ■ Value and inspire them.

- ■ Inject fun and interest into your programme.

- ■ Make giving easy and rewarding.

- ■ Move donors up the pyramid.

- ■ Thank and celebrate support.

- ■ Evaluate and invest.

These are the prime ingredients of a successful individual giving programme.